YOUR KNOWLEDGE HAS VALUE

- We will publish your bachelor's and
  master's thesis, essays and papers

- Your own eBook and book -
  sold worldwide in all relevant shops

- Earn money with each sale

Upload your text at www.GRIN.com
and publish for free

Desirée Kuthe

African American Vernacular English

GRIN Verlag

Bibliografische Information der Deutschen Nationalbibliothek:

Die Deutsche Bibliothek verzeichnet diese Publikation in der Deutschen National-
bibliografie; detaillierte bibliografische Daten sind im Internet über http://dnb.d-
nb.de/ abrufbar.

Imprint:

Copyright © 2007 GRIN Verlag GmbH
Druck und Bindung: Books on Demand GmbH, Norderstedt Germany
ISBN: 978-3-638-84510-6

This book at GRIN:

http://www.grin.com/en/e-book/77753/african-american-vernacular-english

GRIN - Your knowledge has value

Der GRIN Verlag publiziert seit 1998 wissenschaftliche Arbeiten von Studenten, Hochschullehrern und anderen Akademikern als eBook und gedrucktes Buch. Die Verlagswebsite www.grin.com ist die ideale Plattform zur Veröffentlichung von Hausarbeiten, Abschlussarbeiten, wissenschaftlichen Aufsätzen, Dissertationen und Fachbüchern.

Student: Desirée Kuthe

Course: Lingüística aplicada "A" (Sociolingüística del Inglés)

January 2007

AFRICAN AMERICAN VERNACULAR ENGLISH

1. Introduction

African American Vernacular English or AAVE, which is also variously labelled 'African American English', 'Black English', 'Black Vernacular English' or 'Ebonics', is the non-standard variety of English spoken by many African Americans, at least to some extent and in some contexts. The now very popular term Ebonics is a portmanteau of the words ‚ebony' and ‚phonics', created in 1973 by a group of black scholars, who disliked the term 'Nonstandard Negro English', which was in use at that time. The circumstances of the creation of the term, (which has gained considerable popularity during a huge debate in 1996, which will be discussed later), already highlights one of the main features associated with AAVE: the controversies which centre upon it, "even" – according to McCrum et al. –

> "within the Black community. For some, it is an authentic means of self-expression for Black
> English speakers throughout America and the world. For others, who prefer the norms of Standard
> English, Black English represents the disadvantaged past, an obstacle to advancement, something
> better unlearned, denied or forgotten."[1]

The first thorough sociolinguistic study of AAVE was carried out by William Labov in 1968. It was funded by the US Office of Education, which was interested in "the relation between

---

[1] Rober McCrum, William Cran, Robert MacNeil: The story of English. London 1992[2], p. 209.

social dialects and the teaching of English."[2] The problems many Black American children had to acquire thorough reading skills was, in fact, what first brought attention to AAVE. Still scholars can't seem to agree on what exactly AAVE is and where it comes from. Scholars on one end of the scale of opinions hold it to be very different from Standard English, even a distinct language, those on the other end claim it to be a mere product of regional and socio-economical differences between Blacks and Whites.

These two aspects will be the main points of interest in this paper. After a rough linguistic description of the dialect[3] I'm going to turn to its possible history, before finally concluding with a short outline of the main sociolinguistic aspects surrounding AAVE, including the educational problems it presents, which have, after all, been the catalyst for linguistic interest in the dialect.

2. Linguistic Features

According to Ralph W. Fasold, there are three types of features of AAVE – or of any variety of English -, that is: "(1) unmarked features, in the sense that they do not doffer from the corresponding structures in standard English, (2) non-standard features shared with other non-standard varieties, and (3) unique, also non-standard, features."[4]

I will completely leave out the first type of features, as it would fill tomes to describe all the many grammatical and phonological, not to mention the shared lexical items. Of the second category, I will give some examples of the most striking phenomenons[5]. The third category is still being disputed by scholars: Features some of them regard as unique are labelled shared by others. In order not to get carried away, I'm going to present some examples Fasold has thoroughly investigated and, after gathering sufficient evidence, proclaimed as unique.

2.1 Shared non-standard features

A quite striking feature of AAVE is the use of the verb 'to be'. A number of non-standard ways to apply it occur in the dialect: *ain't* for *isn't* (and also sometimes for *didn't* which according to Fasold could even be a unique feature), as well as a lack of concordance in the finite forms of 'to be' in the present tense. A further feature is double negation, especially in sentences with indefinite pronouns like *Ain't nobody like her*. This example is also an

---

[2] Rickford and Rickford, Dialect Readers Revisited, www.edu-cyberpg.com/Linguistics/Dialect_Readers_Revisited.htm, 28.12.2006, 10:58.
[3] That's the term I've chosen for the time being, out of necessity and out of lack of an approved-of term.
[4] Ralph W. Fasold: The Relation between Black and white speech in the south. In: Harold B. Allen / Michael D. Linn: Dialect and language variation, p. 446-473, p. 450.
[5] I have to admit that my choice will probably be highly subjective. Still, I have to make one and I'm therefore going to present those features mentioned by most of the literature I have consulted.

example for a typical change in the word-order, shifting the negated verb to the beginning of the sentence. Further features are the possibility to omit a relative pronoun which functions as a subject in the following relative clause, as for example in: *Show me a nice girl ain't have no boyfriend.*

Examples for shared phonological characteristics are: mergers of vowels, so that pin = pen[6], find = fund [a], fond = fund [a], poor = Poe = door. Further, there may be non-rhoticity, especially after vowels, as well as the deletion or vocalization of postvocalic /l/. The dental fricatives may be pronounced either as /f/ or as /t/ (mouth = mouf, with = wit), the initial unvoiced dental fricative is often stopped, so that then = den.

2.2 Unique non-standard features

Non-standard features Fasold labels as unique are much fewer than those shared by other features, just a few of which are listed above. One of them is the use of *been* in order to indicate a temporarily remote aspect. Fasold claims that there are striking differences not only of the use, but also of the comprehension of sentences such as *She been married* as an answer to *Is she married?* This way to apply been seems to occur only in AAVE and before verbs that are uninflected or in a past tense form.

Another grammatical feature is the absence of the possessive suffix *'s* as well as the absence of the verbal suffix –*s* (in third person singular forms of the present tense) and the plural suffix –*s* of nouns. In a survey Fasold cites a group of "lower-class black children" had no possessive suffixes in 52, 2 percent of the possessive constructions they uttered. I mention this number in order to stress again the fact that the features listed here are definitely not obligatory and can always be substituted by standard realisations. Also, I'd like to stress again that of a similar group of "upper-middle-class black children" just one child used the zero realisation of the possessive suffix, and only once, showing that by no means all African Americans speak AAVE. A further characteristic is frequent omission of present tense forms of *to be*, normally before *gonna* or progressive forms, adjectives or nouns. An example for that characteristic would be *She beautiful*. While *are* is according to Fasold frequently omitted as well by white Southerners, *is* normally appears in the speech of white. The infinitive form of *to be*, on the other hand, is used in a sense unknown to other varieties of English: to indicate that something happens regularly, as in *Sometime he be comin here*. The few white

---

[6] I want to emphasize at this point that none of the features of AAVE are obligatory. In all contexts standard versions may also be chosen, though in more formal contexts this will probably occur more often. In addition, there are variations even within AAVE, as well as different intensities of preferring AAVE forms of standard English forms.

people who use it, according to Fasold, who calls this phenomenon "distributive 'be'" have probably learned it from speakers of AAVE.

A phonological unique feature is a certain way to reduce final consonant clusters. The reduction itself is not unique but typical for almost all varieties of English, even prestige varieties. But the qualitative extend to which it was done in a study by Fasold indicated that even in the underlying mental representations of at least some speakers of AAVE these consonant clusters were simply absent and substituted by simple *s*.

Jack Sidnell also mentions special features of the lexicon, which tend to spread into other varieties of English but nonetheless originate in AAVE: "Any discussion of AAVE vocabulary must take note of the many recent innovations which occur in this variety and which tend to spread rapidly to other varieties of English."[7] Sidnell discerns several types of 'borrowing'[8]: The first one is that of whole lexical items as well as their semantic meaning ("West African form + West African meaning"). One of the examples he gives is *hep, hip*, which means 'well-informed, up to date' and comes from the Wolof expression *hipi, hepi*, meaning 'to open one's eyes, be aware of what is going on'. The second type is an English form which has been semantically 'broadened' by a West African meaning. Examples for this type are *cat*, meaning 'a friend' and coming from the Wolof suffix *–kat*, indicating a person, as well as *bad*, which means 'really good'. Sidnell argues that in many creoles as well as West African languages, the words for 'bad' are used to denote 'good' as well as a booster, a degree adverb which is pointing to a high point on the degree scale, similar to 'very'. The third type of 'borrowing' mentioned is loan-translation. An example would be big-eye, which means 'greedy' and has probably been translated word by word from the Ibo expression anya uku, which also expresses 'covetous' and literally means 'big-eye'.

3. History

The discussion of linguistic features directly lead to the question of the variety's history, as scholars seem to have linked some of those features successfully to a possible ancestor of AAVE: a Creole spoken by the ancestors of modern AAVE-speakers – by slaves, hence

---

[7] Jack Sidnell: African American Vernacular English (Ebonics). <<http://www.une.edu.au/langnet/aave.htm>>, 28.12.2006, 10:17.
[8] I am aware of the fact that the process at hand is not definitely a genuine borrowing process but that the lexical items could also be retained rather than loaned. For lack of a better expression, though, I'm going to refer to 'borrowing'.

sometimes called 'Plantation Creole'[9]. Stewart, according to Wells one of "those who argue strongly for the creole hypothesis"[10], writes in 1968:

> Indeed, the non-standard speech of present-day American Negroes still seems to exhibit structural traces of a creole predecessor, and this is probably a reason why it is in some ways more deviant from Standard English than is the non-standard speech of even the most uneducated American whites.[11]

The most substantial evidence for the Creole hypothesis is provided by some syntactic unique features of AAVE. In fact, three of the characteristics listed above (though one of them is a phonological one) are used by Fasold as support for his thesis of decreolization. First, the probable underlying forms of lexical items ending in consonant clusters, where those are substituted by *s*, indicate that the underlying forms stem from something which is not Standard English. Second, the absence of *to be* forms in African American Vernacular English, according to Fasold, may represent "the remnants of the earlier creole, in which their absence was a syntactic phenomenon." The fact that one form of *to be* (the 2nd singular form *are*) is omitted by white Southern speakers as well can be explained by phonological reduction (Southern American speech tends to be *r*-less). Last, there is the "distributive 'be'"-phenomenon, which seems to exist exclusively in AAVE, apart from the few white Southern speakers who have competence in it and who have probably learned "distributive 'be'" from speakers of AAVE. This phenomenon could be a grammatical feature brought into the Creole by one or several African languages.

Fasold illustrates his decreolization theory with the way consonant cluster reduction may have developed from the original Creole into AAVE. He generally remarks: "What is known about some of those features is consistent with the hypothesis that they arose from a creole language and their current place in VBE grammar can be understood as the result of decreolization."[12] Relating to the particular case of consonant cluster reduction, he claims that creole languages generally tend to avoid consonant clusters in any position, but particularly in final position. As the creole came ever closer to "the standard language from which it derived most of its vocabulary"[13], speakers heard more and more words with final consonant clusters, accepting ever more exceptions and finally having the same lexical items but in tendency with the vague communal 'memory' that final clusters are disallowed. Hence the underlying forms without

---

[9] See for instance McCrum et al.: The history of English, p. 226.
[10] J. C. Wells: Accents of English, Volume III: Beyond the British Isles. Cambridge 1996, p. 555
[11] Ibd.
[12] Fasold, p. 466.
[13] Ibd.

clusters some speakers seem to have. Specifically, Fasold proposes four stages of decreolization, the first of which is the original Creole, where final clusters are disallowed, the fourth modern AAVE, where phonotactics coincide with those of Standard English. The two transitional stages Fasold suggests allow only such clusters ending in [t].

Though he stresses the fact that this model is a hypothesis, he suggests to gather more evidence, remarking: "Present-day VBE may well be an example of what a late postcreole looks like; the study of it can therefore add to our knowledge of creole phenomena."[14]

4. Sociolinguistic aspects

As already indicated in the introduction, several questions around AAVE, even around its mere existence have triggered debates during the second half of the 20th century. One of these debates - that concerning the varieties' origins - has already been discussed above. Two further aspects, which influence not also academics' perception of AAVE but also - being widely discussed in the media of the United States – the speakers themselves, shall be presented in the following: the question of prestige and that of education.

4.1 Prestige

In the introduction to this paper it has already been mentioned, that the question of how prestigious AAVE is comes up again and again. Fasold talks of "a topic with emotional overtones, like race and speech"[15], McCrum et al. claim: "No other form of speech in the history of the English language has been so deplored, debated and defended."[16]

To begin with, before the 1960s, when linguists started to become interested in AAVE – and actually in some cases, it seems, even in the mid nineteen eighties still, when Fasold published his survey – the mere existence of AAVE as a variety of English was seriously questioned. The differences between 'Black speech' and Standard speech (or, more generally, the different varieties spoken by white people) were perceived as "serious cognitive and linguistic deficits"[17], caused by the fact that most speakers of AAVE were (and still are) in tendency socially disadvantaged.

A second aspect concerning prestige is the way in which AAVE is perceived within the Black community itself, which seems to be divided. Again, I'd like to quote McCrum et al.'s comment, that

---

[14] Ibd., p. 469.
[15] Fasold, p. 446.
[16] McCrum et al., p. 210.
[17] Fasold, p. 447.

> For some [members of the Black community], it is an authentic means of self-expression for Black English speakers throughout America and the world. For others, who prefer the norms of Standard English, Black English represents the disadvantaged past, an obstacle to advancement, something better unlearned, denied or forgotten.[18]

There is a second side to the question as well, though. Toni Cook, a member of the Oakland school board who passed a resolution concerning AAVE (to be discussed in the following section), remarks in an interview:

> My youngest daughter has had that criticism: 'You talk like a white girl.' It's another way of saying, 'How come you don't sound like us?' It hurts to be accused of that. When I was a girl, it was a goal to speak Standard English, not a ridicule. I have no idea how that changed.[19]

Obviously, it seems to be difficult for those Black children, who have contact to people speaking Standard English as well as some speaking AAVE, to decide between non-standard and standard speech. Either decision seems to isolate them in particular contexts.

A third aspect which should add to the prestige of the variety is the fact that AAVE has developed a literature. An early example for AAVE poetry is the poem 'Wey Down souf' by Daniel Webster Davis (1862-1913):

O, de birds ar' sweetly singin',

'Wey down Souf,

An' de banjer is a-ringin',

'Wey down Souf;

An' my heart it is a-sighin',

Whil' de moments am a-flyin'

Fur my hom' I am a-cryin',

'Wey down Souf.

An example for contemporary literature including elements of AAVE is that of Toni Morrison, an African-American, Standard English speaking author, who has been awarded the Nobel Prize for Literature. She frequently includes characters in her novels who speak AAVE: "'What'd be the point?' asked Baby Suggs. 'Not a house in the country aint' packed to its rafters with some dead Negro's grief. We lucky this ghost is a baby.'"[20] The fact that AAVE has found entrance to Nobel-Prize winning novels – and not as something to be ridiculed but as the natural speech of the protagonists, as it is – gives reason to assume that though certainly

---

[18] McCrum et al., p. 209.

[19] Nanette Asimov: Sunday Interview - Opening Pandora's Box (January 19, 1997), http://www.sfgate.com/cgi-bin/article.cgi?file=/chronicle/archive/1997/01/19/SC55142.DTL, 28.12.2006, 10:44.

[20] Toni Morrison, Beloved, London 2005[10], p. 6.

still much discussed, the prestige of AAVE has considerably risen since the 1960s, when it was called 'Nonstandard Negro English'.

4.2 Educational issues

As already stated, the linguists' first interest for AAVE in the 1960s was triggered by educational issues. In fact, a group of Black activists wanted schools to 'make allowances' for AAVE-speaking children, accepting it as a standard variety of English for Black people. The argument ran along the lines of "You have recognized the political and social rights of the Blacks, […] now you must recognize their language rights."[21] – making the linguistic matter a political one, linked to the debate about Black rights, in one fell swoop. Instantly, and of course as a consequence of the prestige issue discussed above, many middle-class Blacks distanced themselves from such demands, fearing to decrease their children's future prospectives as well as promoting "the spirit of the ghetto"[22]. As a result, a school district in Detroit was ordered by court decision to take the Black English some schoolchildren spoke into account. Fifteen years later the same topic arose anew, though with less radical demands: The Oakland School Board passed a resolution to acknowledge AAVE as "the primary language of African American children"[23] and, again, to take it into account when planning Language Arts lessons. That resolution led to a second huge debate in the United States.

Several possible approaches to solve that problem have been proposed. Even before the Oakland resolution, several programs to help Black children learn to read had been developed, some of them bidialectal: teaching to read first in the vernacular and then making the transition to Standard English. An example for an AAVE translation of the Bible (John 3:1-17) is:

- Jesus answered him, 'Truly, truly, I say to you, unless one is born anew, he cannot see the kingdom of God.

- Jesus, he tell him say, 'This ain't no jive, if a man ain't born over again, ain' no way he gonna get to know God.

Several scholars, though, report the bidialectal approach to have proven a failure:

Blacks themselves led the opposition to such a move, and teachers, parents, and black activists united to oppose it… Their motives were various: some felt that such readers would disadvantage black children; others denied the validity of the variety of language itself; still others resisted the notion that there should be any defferences at all made in teaching white and black children; and

---

[21] McCrum et al., p. 246.
[22] Ibd., p. 247.
[23] John R. Rickford: The Ebnoics controversy in my backyard: A sociolinguist's experiences and reflections, www.indiana.edu/~reading/ieo/bibs/ebonics.hmtl, 28.12.2006, 10:38.

still others insisted that the problem, if there was one, was ascribable to attitudes, i.e., was a problem of racism, and not a linguistic problem at all.[24]

Thus, what has lead the approach to failure has nothing to do with linguistic problems, with questions of how to teach children, but with the sensitivity surrounding the subject – the same sensitivity which makes AAVE such a controversial variety regarding its prestige. And this sensitivity is probably due to the fact that still, even in the 20th – and probably as well in the 21st – century, and in the middle of the globalization process, how we speak is not just a neglectable little aspect of our lives. Rather, it seems that still how we speak determines who we want to be and consequently who we are.

---

[24] Wardhaugh 1992:340; cited according to John and Angela Rickford, Dialect Readers Revisited, http://www.edu-cyberpg.com/Linguistics/DIALECT_READERS_REVISITED.html, 28.12.2006, 10:52.

5. Literature

ASIMOV, NANETTE: Sunday Interview – Opening Pandora's Box. The Oakland School Board
member principally response ble for the controversial resolution on Ebonics reflects
on several weeks of turmoil (January 19, 1997). http://www.sfgate.com/cgi-
bin/article.cgi?file=/chronicle/archive/1997/01/19/SC55142.DTL, 28.12.2006, 10:44

FASOLD, RALPH W.: The relation between black and white speech in the south. In: Allen,
Harold B. / Linn, Michael D. (Ed.): Dialect and language variation. Orlando 1986

McCRUM, ROBERT / CRAN, WILLIAM / MACNEIL, ROBERT: The story of English. London 1992

MORRISON, TONI: Beloved. London 2005[10]

RICKFORD, JOHN: The Ebonics controversy in my backyard: A sociolinguist's experiences and
reflections. http://www.indiana.edu/~reading/ieo/bibs/ebonics.html, 28.12.2006, 10:58

RICKFORD, JOHN R. / RICKFORD, ANGELA E.: Dialect Readers Revisited. http://www.edu-
cyberpg.com/Linguistics/DIALECT_READERS_REVISITED.html, 28.12.2006,
10:52

SIDNELL, JACK: African American Vernacular English Ebonics).
http://www.une.edu.au/langnet/aave.htm, 28.12.2006, 10:17

WELLS, J. C.: Accents of English III. Beyond the British Isles. Cambridge 1996